MY FAMILY

AND OTHER EXOTIC BEASTS

DENNIS HOLTZ

"….without a constant falsification of
Life…man could not live…."

Nietzsche

TABLE OF CONTENTS

A BOY AND HIS DOG

I come from thoughtful people. Every option is carefully considered and the alternatives painstakingly weighed. Unfortunately, thereafter we inevitably make absurd decisions based upon nothing more than the instinct of lemmings and complete impatience with the process of actually thinking things through to some logical conclusion.

When my darling son moaned pitifully for a pet when he was about 8, there was every reason to wait since we had just moved from the city to the suburbs and we were like Moses in the Bible: a stranger in a strange land. We realized the importance of my son's acclimating himself to a new school and new friends. We never had a pet before so we had to train ourselves before we could train an animal. We had no idea what breed would make a good family pet and what breed would rip out our throats and steal the silver. Then one day we simply went out and bought the first

dog that jumped up in his cage and barked at us
with such enthusiasm that you would think we
were the coming of the Kibble god. We named
the large Irish setter Eric the Red in honor of my
wife's Scandinavian ancestors.

Having proven once again that we were impulsive
oafs, I, and I alone, compounded our error by
refusing to have him "fixed." As I stood facing
the kindly veterinarian, who had just explained
exactly what "fixing' was, I knew, just as surely as
I was clutching my balls, that it was WRONG to
"fix" any male by removing the family jewels
from the vault. I knew.

In the annals of family mistakes, this one proved
to rank, in every sense of the word, among the top
ten. Our little puppy grew up to deserve top
billing on any Megan's Law site. Listing his
known conquests would cause cardiac arrest in
any would-be Leporello. But his greatest moment

should be memorialized.

Our town consisted in the main of families whose children felt deprived because they were forced to accept their parents' two year old BMWs upon reaching driving age. The B's, the family in the house three doors down our street, were a distinct exception. In the first place, there were nine children; in the second place, some of the children would actually do chores for their family and others, including us, activities that the BMW driving set found repugnant.

One day, Mrs. B called to apologize. She said she knew that she should have had her little puppy spayed but she had been so busy. Would I be so kind as to come to her house for Eric? When I arrived I found that I should have been the one apologizing as our sixty-seven pound bundle of love had jumped their fence to assault the virtue of a seven pound terrier who could no longer wear white. On the long walk home, the wretch showed no signs of remorse: indeed, if a dog could be said to sashay, Eric the Killer shassshayed home with all the pride of the Don Juan of dogdom.

But this was just the prelude to his greatest moment. We had heard that Mrs. B had purchased a goat; in our neighborhood, such news traveled fast and furiously. The assertion that she made this purchase for her children who were allergic to cow's milk was treated with the contempt it deserved; let them drink a modest Burgundy, they declared. Nevertheless, zoning laws being what they were, the goat stayed.

Several months later, I received another call from Mrs. B, but this time the spirit of "hi neighbor" was decidedly lacking: just a terse and icy, "Come over here now. Your dog is on my goat." I grabbed my son and we sprinted to Mrs. B's house while discussing the meaning of the term "your dog is <u>on</u> my goat." Bordering? Near? Adjacent to? Close to? Advancing? Leaning on?

We ran up to the front door but we heard such a loud noise in the rear that we ran to her back yard. What was it we wondered? Ble…AT, Ble…AT, BLE…AT!! BLE….ATT!!

When we arrived we realized that "On" meant "Situated Upon" as we beheld the sight of our boy with his front paws firmly clasped around the chest of his new conquest and his back paws three inches off the ground as the tall, very tall, capricious Capra ran around in a circle giving him the ride of his life. Every time she leaped forward, his hindquarters flew back a few inches; every time she landed, he was thrust forward, she squealed and she leaped forward again.

Eric had a rather bemused expression: he knew that he was doing something extraordinary; he just

wasn't sure what it was. We would have stood
and watched this beastly bacchanalia for a while
but Mrs. B and her goat had joined in a cry for
freedom that rivaled the Israelites in Nabucco so
we reluctantly parted them with a sea of water
from the garden hose.

We muttered our apologies and slunk off dragging
our ravishing reprobate. This time he did the stroll
all the way home puffing on an imaginary
cigarette while acknowledging his adoring
audience with a careless wave of his right front
paw.

For the rest of his life, we never wondered what he
was dreaming of when he stirred in his sleep as all
dogs occasionally do: we knew that the bastard
was reliving his very own afternoon of a faun.

A MOTHER'S LOVE

Now my family is known for their extraordinary fidelity to the truth: not only do they always tell the unvarnished truth, they do not exaggerate, embellish, embroider or even overstate (although they occasionally understate out of a sense of modesty that does them credit). The following is the true story.

I was raised by my grandmother: while my parents, my grandparents and I all lived together in a little house in Brooklyn, I was most assuredly raised by my grandmother; she made me breakfast as my mother slept, she made me lunch as my mother attended a luncheon to raise money for the Free Nurses, a popular charity in 1944, and she tucked me in at night as my mother attended some social function for yet another charity. On Saturday, my Mother arose early and took her weekly pilgrimage to the fabled emporium known as Bloomingdale's.

When one of my mother's many sisters chastised her for her evident lack of attention to her only son, my mother decided, with her usually efficiency, to join duty to pleasure and bring me along on her weekly jaunts to the then most elegant of department stores.As she hustled from sales items to close-outs to bargains, she grew so tired of dragging me on legs too short to do more than scurry that she soon dumped me on a display couch with an arm-load of books and, with a stare that could paralyze a basilisk, ordered me to sit still until she returned. With her usual economy, she did not add "like a good boy" as neither of us was under any illusion about the other. So I sat and I read my favorite books: "Bambi", "Little Sambo" and a version of "Alice in Wonderland" suitable for a five year old. I was happy to sit there and read while my mother was smugly satisfied to fulfill whatever few maternal duties society imposed and she reluctantly acknowledged.

I do not remember how long this maternal marathon continued, I can only remember the last visit. One day, as I sat quietly reading, the serpent of hunger gently wafted the alluring aroma of hot dogs in my general direction and then assured me that my need for food was greater than the fear my mother had tried to instill in me. It was probably the same for Eve in the Garden of Eden (although at no time did God appear in Bloomingdale's, at least not to me). I followed that delicious smell to a nearby faux soda fountain that Bloomies had recently installed in a fit of whimsy. With no small difficulty, I ascended one of the red leather stools and waited while using my hands to turn in one direction and then the other, and then in the other and then in the other, ad infinitum and ad nauseum. My reverie was rudely interrupted by a short-fat, white haired woman, dressed in a pink uniform that was neither befitting nor appropriate for one who was blessed with great age and a body with no discernable shape: she did, however, had a face like an irritated Pekinese and a bark to match. She suggested that I stop rotating in a voice that was redolent of drill sergeants and dictators: I stopped. She then asked what I wanted.

"A hot dog, please," I whined.
"Do you have money?" she asked.

When I relied no, she asked where my mother was. In deference to my heritage alluded to above, I could only answer truthfully: I had no idea. She began to cross

examine me with the vigor and skill of a
Perry Mason and it did not take long for her
to extract from a not too bright child that I
was abandoned each and every Saturday,
"over there" as I pointed vaguely in the
direction of "my couch" and my books.

Now is now but that was then and Mrs.
Pekinese felt obligated to feed me a hot dog
and a "chalklet" milkshake before she called
security, the police, child welfare and
any other institution she could think of.
Well, my mother appeared before I finished
stuffing my fat and now happy face. She
was livid: I told you not to move she hissed.
My guard dog attacked: "You have some
hell of a nerve, lady, leaving a little kid by
himself in this place. I should report you to
the police." "He is perfectly ok as long as he
has enough to read. And it is none of your
business."

Parry, thrust. I ate my hot dog, drank my milkshake and watched two heavy-weight New Yorkers verbally duke it out without fear or even embarrassment. I have since seen Ali fight Holmes in the Trilla in Manilla but they could not compare to the Mother versus the Waitress that morning.

I finished my meal and wandered back to my couch and my books as they continued their confrontation. After a few minutes, my mother marched over, slightly red in the face and breathing a little hard but unfazed, unbowed and unrepentant.

On the subway home, the only thing she said was, "I told you not to move." I still think about it but I am pretty sure that it is too late now for me to call Child Services.

CHEZ MA MERE

My family professed reverence for their elders with such Nipponese enthusiasm that it is with some sense of guilt that I confess that we frequently referred to my mother as "Ludicrous Borgia", "The Kiss of Death" and "The Hand that Nauseates the Cradle" for her culinary skills.

During her childhood, she was able to escape any kitchen experience except eating by cleverly choosing a family that could afford a cook. She continued such avoidance by marrying a man whose mother enjoyed dazzling her family three times a day with feasts that would fill the eyes of any Cordon Bleu chef with tears of envy. Unfortunately for her, and us, we were expelled from this foodie paradise when we moved from the ancestral home and left my grandma sadly waving her apron goodbye.

It is only fair to note that after our move, her leisure time was as meager as our budget so she became a pioneer of meals unpacked rather than prepared.   Items on sale, such as American cheese and bologna on day old bread, made their appearance with monotonous regularity.

Her first foray into a world where you actually turned on an oven was the result of such a sale: three cans of blueberries for the price of one and a free frozen pie-shell in its own little tin foil pan. With her usual efficiency, immediately after dinner she opened one can, poured it into the still frozen pie shell, popped her product into the oven with the type of hope that springs from complete ignorance and then, and only then, did she turn on the oven to high. Long, long after dinner, we smelled the stench of burnt pie shell and she insisted that we return to the dinner table. There, in the center of the table, was a strange sight: one half of the scalloped top of the pie shell was black while the other side was a pasty white, the bottom of the pie shell was no longer frozen but neither had it cooked, and in the middle bubbled a strange purplish, lumpy soup. "Bubble, bubble, toil and trouble", muttered my high school sister, as we reluctantly sat down.

My mother could only apportion her production by

pouring the filling in another bowl, chisel out shards of pie shell, dumping them in soup plates and ladling out a generous portion in the bowls. Everyone subtlety but firmly pushed back as my mother pushed the bowls towards us until my father , the hypocrite, boomed "Looks great, dear", as if sheer volume could beat the other senses into submission. He did prove to be brave as well as gracious by actually taking a bite of this admixture, but, despite his best efforts, his smile began to slip into a grimace as he realized that my mother did not know that sugar was a necessary component of blueberry pie. His glare forced us into an equal act of foolhardiness: then we fled the table as quickly as the Jews had left Egypt but even hungrier

Now every narrator finds himself tossed between the Charybdis of truthfulness and Scylla of good taste. Therefore, after noting that we had but one bathroom, I will only say that late that evening there occurred in our home a religious fervor that had not been seen since the Second Great Awakening: sincere and heartfelt cries of

"Oh, God", "God help me" and "Dear God" filled the air.

This incident was treated by my mother, with barely concealed contempt, as just another example of our lack of will power and our inability to "make do." But she was too intelligent not to quickly recognize that her true talent lay in the field of combining ingredients that had been prepared by others: Campbell's, Chef Boy-R-Dee and others of their ilk. Unfortunately, her pride would not let her leave well enough alone: she dubbed her new found skill as "doctoring it up." For example, she truly believed that a can of noodle soup was raised from the mundane to the miraculous by the addition of a galoop of ketchup. Who else would have thought of dipping chicken tenders into a jar of honey and baking them until they turned mahogany in taste and texture?

Opportunity and inclination had its most glorious meeting when our local banks began to offer a cheap kitchen appliance each time you opened a new account. The woman was relentless and soon we had a score of accounts at various banks (each with the minimum balance, of course), and our kitchen counters were covered by a sea of toasters, mixers, blenders, electric knives and can openers.

Her pride and joy, the ladder she intended to climb to new heights of culinary achievements, was the then new toaster oven: a device that promised no fuss and, more importantly, no muss. She soon became the absolute monarch of meals that merely required the opening of a package and the choosing between broil, bake or toast. Unfortunately, we all know that pride goeth before a fall and one day Ma Mere decided that she could make spare ribs in her new toy. She carefully spread silver foil on the tray, lay the ribs on the foil, placed the tray on its highest position, turned the dial and left to go shopping. The apartment was empty except for my father who was taking a nap in his Lazy Boy.

Now I must interrupt this exciting narrative to tell you that my father had no use of his legs due to MS but while he was weak in the locomotion department, his gift for epic dramatization was still strong. According to him, the first hint that something was amiss was when thick black smoke poured from the kitchen and filled the living room until he could no longer see his wheel chair standing in front of him. Notwithstanding no legs, and now no eyes, he grabbed the wheelchair, flung himself in with the strength of the soon to be cooked, wheeled himself to the front door that he found by sheer animal instinct, and then pushed himself down a long corridor to the elevator to heroically warn the other tenants of his wife's attempt to fry them all.

Notwithstanding the fact that the Fire Department found little more than a carbonized toaster oven and a black wall behind it, my mother reluctantly agreed that dining out for the rest of their lives had a certain appeal. But every once in a while in the years to follow, my mother would wander into the kitchen, cradle one of her little kitchen appliances in her arms and whisper to herself: "I could have been a contender."

EVEN MORE MOTHER'S LOVE

Most modern American families seem to have an overabundance of hobbies. We all seem to lurch from one leisure time activity to another. My Mother was different. She devoted every moment to one activity and only one activity- money. I hasten to add that this did not represent greed or avarice. It did not even reflect need. It was simply a sport that she played for the sheer love of the game. It was the Platonic ideal of striving for perfection knowing that perfection was not possible (perfection being, of course, having all of the money in the world). And it was irrelevant whether you scored by acquisition of income or by diminution of expense; both resulting in the only thing that mattered- more.

Given this background, you should not be surprised to know that I worked every summer of my life, beginning the day after school ended and ending the day before school began (unfortunately, you had to buy some new clothing

and school supplies sometime). Near the end of
my senior year in high school, my Mother handed
me an envelope containing, she told me, "Your
birthday present." Since I had always received the
same thoughtful personal gift from her, a check
that she promptly took back to deposit in my
college fund, I was shocked to discover that this
envelope contained an airline ticket: LaGuardia to
Paris on Icelandic Airlines. When I expressed my
astonishment, my Mother assured me that this
present was not the result of a visit by the Ghost of
Christmas to Come but the bargain of a lifetime.
It seemed that I had received a copy of the Daily
Pennsylvania as an incoming freshman and, since
it was free, she perused it and found that in 1959
you could purchase a round trip ticket for $85.

My Father frequently observed that if horse shit
was half priced, we would be swimming in it, as
his wife was simply not capable of passing up a
bargain. Nevertheless, I was moved. In fact I was

so moved that it took me a while to ask what I would do for money in France. My Mother responded that she had purchased the ticket and any further demands upon her generosity would be both unseemly and unavailing. The week before my adventure, my Father, god bless him, slipped me two $50 bills with a warning to keep silent.

The reason for the low fare was simple: Icelandic was desperately trying to convince potential passengers of the stoic Scandinavian sort that a trip in an ancient jet that made two stops, and therefore took twelve hours, was preferable to a hoity toity new jet that made the trip in a too-hasty six hours.

I have always blamed Icelandic Airways for what happened next. When I arrived in the City of Lights at 3:00AM, I was too tired from the long voyage to sleep, so I took a brisk walk. Perhaps it was the hour, perhaps it was the spirit of <u>bon</u>

homme, perhaps it was the beautiful summer night, but in any event everyone greeted me and I cheerfully acknowledged every greeting. "Mon Dieu, qu'est –ce qu'il fout, faire promenade a cette heure?" and "Allons le voler, il a l'aird un vraicon" were met with a joyful "Greetings, what a beautiful city you have."

That spirit seemed to have fled when I awoke in the hospital having apparently traded a lovely lump on my skull for my wallet, passport and watch. Mon Dieu, indeed.

I quickly discovered that before the European Union, a man without a passport was a man without a country. I also discovered that a new passport took six weeks to process. Finally, I discovered that the U.S. Embassy had taken a page from my dear Mother's notes from the underworld and told me in no uncertain terms that it found the idea that they should advance funds was not only unseemly and unavailing but even faintly amusing.

In a moment of great generosity, they allowed me to use one of their phones to call my home collect. To this day, my Mother insists, with wide-eyed innocence, that when she received the call she misunderstood the operator and thought that someone was calling ME collect rather than me calling HER collect so her refusal to accept the charges was reasonable under the circumstances.

My education continued apace as I learned that there was no employment in France for a young student and student hostels could be quite hostile to the impoverished. I had been told that if I was desperate enough I could always hitch hike to Scandinavia as the farmers there hired field hands with or without papers for the very short harvest season. Having the geographical sense that led to the discovery of India by Columbus, I decided that

I could reach Norway in a day or two and earn enough to vacation in style until my passport was issued.

2,703 kilometers and nine days later, I reached Trondheim, Norway, fifty miles south of the Arctic Circle, where I secured a sinecure as a "skit streber" for "forty kroner" plus room and board. Wow. To take in the sag in this saga, instead of a detailed description of the next six weeks, which would only bring copious tears to your eyes, you may simply imagine Charles Dickens rewriting "Hard Times" to substitute a short, formerly pudgy New Yorker and a Scandinavia farm. You'll get the general idea.

After six weeks I accumulated enough for a train ticket to Paris and at least a few days room and board. I should have said just enough for I arrived at LaGuardia airport a week later without a penny and had to hitchhike to our apartment in New

Jersey. I arrived a little after 9:00 PM. As I gazed up at the familiar front canopy in the twilight, I was filled with a deep sense of satisfaction: "well done little man, you survived."

I ran up the three flights of stairs, too eager to see my beloved parents, my home, a shower, a meal, to use the elevator. I put my key in the lock and turned but the door did not open. I tried again. I would have tried a third time but the door opened and an ancient crone opened the door a crack and stared at me with one baleful eye.

"Who are you?" I gasped.

"Who are you?" she replied.

"I live here," I snapped back.

"No", she snapped back even snappier, "I live here!"

I stared at the number on the door but it was my apartment. I was about to inform her of my confirmation when comprehension cleared her elderly countenance and she muttered: "Oh, they moved. Your mother said you would turn up. She left a number."

She slammed the door shut. I heard the sounds of an arthritic shuffle. A few moments later, the door opened again, a palsied hand flung a scrap of paper in my general direction and the door was slammed shut again. I glanced at the paper. At least it was the same area code but I did not have a dime to activate a payphone. Deciding that desperation topped dignity every time, I gently knocked on the door while rearranging my face to resemble David Copperfield at his most winsome. But when she opened the door a crack, and I asked, in my sweetest voice, to use her phone to call my dear mother, she hissed "No" and "Stop bothering me."

I wandered around until I spotted the local volunteer fire department. One of the volunteers, after laughing and laughing, agreed that parents moving without informing their children constituted an emergency and let me use their phone to call the new number.

I would like to conclude by telling you that my mother was deeply repentant but her only reaction was, and I quote, "So why didn't you call before?"

THE WEDDING

I was raised in a household devoid of religion. When I visited the homes of neighbors, friends or relatives I always assumed that the pictures of smug women holding radioactive babies and giant candleholders decorated with six-pointed stars and the like were simply the result of unfortunate decorating choices.

My paradise of spiritual obliviousness abruptly ended in 1957 when my parents moved from New York City to a small town in the wilds of South Jersey in the middle of my freshman year in high school. My new school required its students to read a Biblical verse of their own choosing after saluting the flag and singing a rousing version of god bless America. I was stunned. I was appalled. But I did bask in the sun of my own sophistication and sneered at the poor sheep who were chosen each morning to bleat from the Bible as the rest of the class giggled and snorted.

Why I thought that the torch would never be passed to me I cannot recall; probably ignorance and arrogance, my favorite companions to this day. On a rainy Wednesday morning in the third week of my exile, my home room teacher, all four foot ten of her armored, as usual, in a dark blue woolen suit and topped with steel gray hair braided around her head like a war helmet, croaked that she was going out of alphabetic order to give me, as the new student, the opportunity to read the Bible tomorrow. I responded, in the most respectfully tones of which I was capable, that I was an atheist and would prefer not to read the Bible. Given my city of origin, the fabled Sodom and Gomorrah to these cretins, and my own snotty attitude, the class was torn between the joy of watching me executed and the novelty of someone actually refusing an order from such a fearsome authority.

Now you would think that the dullest educator would realize that ordering a child who detested school not to attend school was as effective as a punishment as throwing Brer Rabbit in the briar patch. You would be wrong as I learned that morning when I was suspended until I was "ready to read." I did not waste this wonderful gift. Every morning for the next two weeks, I dressed, ate breakfast with my parental units, walked to school and chatted with my friends until the first bell rung and the poor bastards who were not clever enough to achieve suspension were forced to go to class. I then went home, watched TV and smoked until noon when I returned to school to eat lunch with and mock my classmates.

This vacation ended when my mother came home early one Friday to find me on the couch well before school could have possibly ended. I guess that the continual consumption of cartons of Marlboros decreased the oxygen in my devious brain and my normal ability to reflexively fabricate a story. In any event, I took the high road on this one occasion (a mistake I would never repeat) and I proclaimed that I would not be bullied into breaching the sacred wall separating church and state. My mother promptly perp walked me back to the vice-principal in charge of discipline at school and assured him that on Monday, I would read. I must pause to confess that my mother intimidated me. I was quite sure that expressions such as "or I'll kill you" were, in her case at least vis-a-vis me, not a mere threat but a statement of fact. She made it clear on numerous occasions that she did not like me well enough to deal with teenage angst or anguish.

I have few virtues and less talents but I was always an unusually rapid reader. So on Friday night I borrowed a Gideon bible from a neighbor and began to read. If I had to read a passage of the damn thing, I wanted something worthwhile. I hate to confess that I loved this book: the stories were fascinating and I learned scores of quotations and references which I never knew were biblical. Sunday morning I read Matthew and found the mot juste: divine inspiration undoubtedly.

On Monday morning, I actually dressed in something other than dungarees and a sweatshirt for my debut as a biblical scholar. I considered a large crucifix or a yarmulke but since neither was available in our house, I made do with my own Bible and a deeply spiritual countenance. The pledge of allegiance and god bless America were even more perfunctory than usual as everyone waited for me to be brought to heel. I stood, opened my Bible to page 991 and began.

I lulled my teacher into a false sense of security with a gentle beginning: "The book of the generation of Jesus Christ, the son of David, the son of Abraham." Just when she thought she won, I hit her with: "Abraham BEGAT Issac." In case my emphatic emphasis was insufficient for the dunderheads, I paused after each "BEGATE" and winked at the class. The brighter ones began to titter. I continued. "And Isaac BEGAT Jacob." Pause and wink. The titters turned to laughter even though as my teacher "SHHHed" like a tea kettle gone rogue. To the whistles and applauds of my classmates, I got up to "And Jacob BEGAT" when my teacher ripped the Bible out of my hand and ordered me to sit down. I could not resist: "Madam, I was suspended for refusing to read and now you don't want me to read. I am so confused."

About now you may be wondering what the hell does this have to do with my wedding. I will now tell you, impatient reader. Many years later, I fell in love with a lovely young Swedish girl. A blond hair, blue-eyed daughter of the North whose passport may have had Lutheran under religion but proved to be as Jewish as Golda Mier. A Scandinavian princess who measured current events with the ruler "Is it good for the Jews?" I should not have been surprised, but I was, when she announced, shortly after our engagement, that she had signed us up for a "conversion class." "Conversion to what?" I protested but the next week I found myself in the parking lot of Beth Something or Other. For you see, after some disgusting and demeaning begging on my part, My Bride had finally agreed that if I drove her to class, I could stay in the car and read. It was the same conclusion my mother had come to years before: I was marginally less of a pain in the ass if I was allowed to sit quietly and read. Unfortunately, five or ten minutes later, My Treasure interrupted my reading by tapping on the window and announcing that HER RABBI insisted upon both parties attending the class. I took my book and found a seat as far back in the class as possible. My beloved was happy, I, quietly reading, was happy: life was good. It continued to be good until I overheard an explanation of why Jews do not eat pork. To make an overly long story a little shorter, a spirited discussion ensued. The rabbi slandered the pig as unclean; the goyem, led by yours truly, responded that today our porcine brothers had less trichinosis then cattle, citing a recent article in Scientific America. The rabbi had dealt with the unclean before so he was quick to cite the need for the teachers, known as rabbis, to separate the chosen people, citing the bible; the unchosen noted that such segregation ensured a continual supply of financial support for the segregationists, citing Karl Marx. Unfortunately such an intellectual exchange of ideas was interrupted by the bell signifying the end of class. On the way out I was just telling my bride-to- be what an exhilarating experience conversion class turned out to be when the good rabbi threw a companionable arm over my shoulder and suggested that I could stay in the parking lot in the future. He also suggested that my beloved should consider dating "a nice Jewish boy.

My fiancé had told me when I proposed that her only condition was that her beloved brother had to be present to "give her away." From early August to the middle of December, try as she might, the irresistible sister was unable to force the immovable brother to commit to a date certain. Finally, on a Tuesday night in the third week of December, my parents convinced her to set the date in February so they would have the time to organize the wedding. When we arrived at our apartment late that night, the telephone was ringing and the bride-to-be in February answered and began speaking in her native tongue. I noticed that as the conversation grew longer and longer, her voice grew louder and louder. She finally slammed down the receiver, turned to me and announced that her brother had a business meeting in our city on Friday and we were getting married that weekend.

As I was trying to remove my jaw from my chest where it came to rest, my beloved was calling HER RABBI to ask him to officiate at the nuptials although the want-to-be was not yet the be. If the conversation with her brother in her native tongue was confusing, her conversation with HER RABBI was worse. Words like "chupah ", "ketubah" and " shagust", appeared and disappeared like brightly colored pebbles in a swiftly flowing stream. Apparently, there was an agreement being negotiated of which I was a subject if not a participant. The rabbi's apprentice smirked as she hung up the phone and said: "He agreed to marry us this weekend but you cannot break the glass." In a triumph of ecumenical enthusiasm, I readily agreed even I was not entirely sure what the hell was going on.

Three and one half days later, I found myself in full wedding regalia greeting guests in front of the same chapel my sister had been married five years ago. Although I was nervous at first, I was able to talk to some of the guests. My sister and I commiserated about her recent divorce and both of us sympathized with my cousin whose husband had died in Nam a few months before.

But I soon became parched from nerves and the night before. I decided to have an orange juice but the helpful bartender added a little champagne: a mimosa, he said. The first was good. The second was better. The third was magnificent but I seemed to lose the ability to count. The next thing I know I was escorted into a room with a great deal of people and told to walk towards HER RABBI and wait. I complied as I was now more compliant as I had ever been before. The milk of human kindness positively coursed through my veins as I looked around at the friends and family who had come to celebrate this magnificent occasion. My eyes grew moist as with gratitude at the thought that upon three days' notice, three lousy days' notice, they had dropped everything to be here.

Just then my bride walked down the aisle on the arms of her brother: an angel in white. She stopped half way and her brother turned and sat down. The Rabbi hissed "Go get her" and I started to. Just then my sister and my cousin began to cry. Loudly. Very, very loudly. From the end of the 14th century when the Church in Ireland outlawed professional mourners (known as keeners) to te date of our wedding, there had never been such a weeping and wailing at a religious ceremony. Indeed, some survivors of this ceremony later told me that the sounds emanating from my dear sister and cousin were so loud that they began to suspect that at least one of us was being lead down the aisle involuntarily. Another survivor compared the noise to the outpouring of grief by French aristocracy as their loved ones passed in tumbrels on the way to the guillotine. My beloved was holding a large bouquet of fresh wild flowers half way down the aisle. When the Furies began their chorus, she began to quiver so strenuously that the flowers sounded like aspens in a mountain windstorm in late Fall. By the time we arrived at the podium, we began our married life with the blessing of perfect harmony of thought: WHAT THE HELL WERE WE GETTING INTO?

You would think that after our marriage experience, my wife would have sworn off religious ceremonies forever.

Unfortunately, her stubbornness far exceeded her memory. During her first pregnancy, she read that that there were fewer complications from circumcisions performed by a specially trained rabbi known as a "mohel." So despite my horror of religious ceremonies and the fact that such a rite would cost much, much more than a quick cut by a resident in the hospital, my wife scheduled my son for a "bris" in our apartment, eight days after his birth.

That day, on the dot of one, a small, dark strange man appeared at our door. He was clad entirely in black. He wore a large somber fedora that was held up only by his ears and a set of muttonchops that would not have been out of place on an 18th century English cavalry officer. Beneath his dusky overcoat he wore a luxurious salt and pepper beard that seemed to reach to his waist. He muttered "mohel" without once looking up and sidled in although the door was not fully opened. When he reached the living room, he muttered "table" and waited until we opened a bridge table and a chair. He sat down and reached into an enormous Gladstone (black, of course) and pulled out an old fashioned ink pen and a linen parchment that covered the table. Without once looking anyone in the eye, he began to ask the pertinent questions beginning with my name. I politely responded until he asked "Hebrew name?" With the speed and agility that quite belied her age, my mother suddenly appeared at my side to shout "Sve." Who knew: I seemed to have another and infinitely more exotic name. My admiration for the old girl turned to awe as she invented Hebrew names for my Swedish wife and the first name of my son. His middle name was her downfall. The Northern Olof does not easily translate into any Middle Eastern tongue and even she hesitated. At that moment, the mohel finally lifted his head, looked at my Valkyian bride and asked "Are you people Jewish?" A short time later I proved my lack of heritage by swooning as he began to snip and the blood began to flow.

Based upon the above, my will clearly states that my funeral shall include no religious ceremony whatsoever.

Based upon the above, I am quite sure that my wife will arrange one and it will be quite an occasion. I am even a little sorry that I will be unable to attend.

BIRTH: A CONFESSION

I have grown tired of being told that my wife is a saint: I understand the not so subtle subtext that I am a pain in the ass and quite beyond any hope of redemption. I would protest if it was not for two incidents in our marriage that have convinced me that they might be, just might be, correct.

The miracle of birth is one that should be celebrated in a Delphic temple where men are excluded under penalty of death. The forces of modern convention can place a man in the birthing room with a camera but he is as necessary as tits on a boar hog and just as attractive.

In a perfect world, which only exists in my imagination, birth would be occur in a shiny white auditorium where beautiful virgins draped in white saris would danced around the birth mother, who is tastefully covered with a white sheet, and then a little bundle of joy would suddenly appear. A window would magically appear, the virgins would hold up the BOJ and the father, safely and sanitarily on the other side of the window, would give an approving nod and go home to watch something on the tube and recover from the trauma. The difference between my imagination and reality has always been substantial. In the case of the birth process, the gulf was so vast that it gave width envy to the Grand Canyon.

In my perfect world, the process of delivering the birth mother to the care of the vestal virgins is vague. In the real world, the process was explained and reexplained by elderly Doctor Winterhaur. He smiled and assured me that even though he could not be there for the delivery, since he was recovering from a heart attack, his young partner, Doctor Medsen, was a wiz and everything would be FINE. He gave me a telephone number on a sheet of paper that clearly specified that we should call that number when the CON TRAC SHUNS were TWO minutes apart.

I must admit that I was slightly annoyed by the tone of these instructions. I was an adult. I was a professional. I was not a child. I could read. And I would prove it.

Several months later (or perhaps years, the memory is thankfully fading), I was awoke to find my darling getting out of bed and making little mewing sounds on her way to the bathroom. Since my wife is of strong Scandinavian stock that shuns any show of emotion, I knew that B Day had arrived! And I was ready!!! I leaped out of bed like a kangaroo on uppers, dialed the number while at the very same time grabbing the birthing bag that contained all of the things that my beloved would need for her visit, while at the same time getting dressed myself. A multi-tasking maniac, I thought proudly.

Suddenly a tired voice muttered: "Yes?" I

responded loudly:" MADISON. MADISON??"
The voice muttered, "No", and hung up.

I was not to be denied. I carefully redialed on the
off-chance that I had misdialed. The same tired
voice snarled:" Yes?" and I again screamed"
MADISON, MADISON!?!? This time he simply
hung up.

When the going gets tough, the tough simply get
tougher. I looked at the instructions and to my
surprise a new paragraph appeared: "In the event
of a DIRE emergency, and we mean DIRE you
idiot, you may call the following number (but only
in the event of a DIRE EMERGENCY,
understand)."

Ha, I thought, who would have thought that I
would be so cool and collected in this DIRE
EMERGENCY, as I dialed the number, which

seemed strangely familiar. The voice on the other side also seemed strangely familiar as I once again yelled, "MADISON, MADISON."

This time my telephone correspondent asked: "WHO THE GOD DAMN HELL ARE YOU CALLING??"
"DOCTOR MADISON, DOCTOR MADISON!!!!"

"DO YOU MEAN DOCTOR MEDSEN, YOU IDIOT."

"Oh, yeah, Medsen", I muttered. "How did you know?"

"BECAUSE I AM DOCTOR WINTERHAUR AND YOU ARE CALLING THE EMERGENCY NUMBER. WHAT IS WRONG??"

"My wife is having contractions."

"How far apart?"

"Oh, I'm not sure. Should I ask her?"

Well, to make a long story short, all was well that ended well: an adorable boy was delivered that night. I would have gone to his office to thank Doctor Medsen but the injunction clearly states that I was barred from telephoning or coming within one hundred feet of any member of their practice. Talk about people who are unable to forgive and forget!

REBIRTH: YET ANOTHER CONFESSION

When my darling announced that she might be
pregnant again by projectile barfing at 4:00AM
one morning, I vowed that I would not repeat the
embarrassing incidents that marred her first
delivery. I would be calm and collected. It would
be easy. Heck, I had been a father for almost three
years. I had actually watched my wife change
diapers filled with the foulest substances known to
man (and woman). This time I knew what was
expected of me: I would be a rock, a pillar of
strength.

And it began well. I had arranged for my mother
to drive to our new apartment and watch the little
prince while I drove the expectant one to the
hospital. We practiced this maneuver until we
resembled a Soviet relay team, smoothly handing
off vehicle and child.

I did not panic when the contractions were five

minutes apart. I suavely called my Mamma and told her that game was afoot. I did not call kindly Doctor Winteraur or not so kindly Doctor Medsen (formerly known as Madison); I called the answering service when the contractions were two minutes apart. I not only had her bag packed and ready to go but I had my own bag of books, puzzles and snacks. As far as I was concerned the only thing missing was an audience to admire the new me in action. Man, was I cool.

My mother drove up in front of our lobby and I maneuvered my beloved into the front passenger seat. I did so with the panache of a born boulevardier although the third trimester had made a skinnier version of Kate Moss look like she had swallowed a Volkswagen.

We slowly drove to the hospital, a matter of seven city blocks east and two blocks north. The City was still, not a pedestrian or another car could be seen but I drove slowly, stopping at every light. It was as if the City was waiting for the birth of our second child with bated breath.

When we pulled in front of the emergency entrance, the only thing that could be seen was the blinking of a red light over the door, softened by the morning mist. I idly thought it resembled the beginning of a recent horror film.

I took a wheelchair and pushed the patient to the front desk wearing the imbecilic grin of a father to be again. The first moment of disquiet occurred when the duty nurse informed me that I had to move my car now. I protested that I was to be an integral part of the birth process this time but the nurse assured me that my wife would be resting in Room 504 and the entire medical institution would stop and wait patiently for my return.

Perhaps the old me would have argued but the new me did not. I leaped into the car and drove away, in no particular direction. You know that there is not very much opened at that time of the morning. As I drove down 8th Street, I noticed that all of the indoor parking lots were closed. As I turned right on Locust Street, I noticed that every legal parking space was filled by some thoughtless residents. As I turned right on 8th Street, I spied with my little eye a light. Aha! There was an outdoor lot on the right side of the street and it was open. The only car on 8th Street was parked a few feet from the entrance to the lot. Continuing my campaign of safety first, I carefully swung the front of my car to the left and then to the right and directly into the side of that peacefully parked car.

Now my life has consisted of lurching from one minor disaster to another so I have had a lot of practice, and I mean a lot of practice, making up excuses, explanations and rationalizations. Despite repeated attempts, I have never been able to explain or excuse smashing into a parked car at

4 AM while trying to enter a parking lot. And I have tried. Lord knows, I have tried.

But that was not even the worse part of this story. No, the worst part is that when I tried to give my license to the attendant so he could tell the owner of the former unmarked vehicle what occurred, the attendant refused my offer: "NO WAY. THAT'LL TEACH THAT MOTHER F___ER TO PARK IN THE STREET. F___ 'IM."

I tried to borrow a pencil and paper to leave a note and got the same response, just louder and ending with "THAT MOTHER DESERVED IT!!"

 I am certain that a moment of reflection would have resulted in a solution but I had not a moment: I knew that without me the entire birthing process would grind to a horrible halt so I ran to the hospital. The elevators were to slow for this so I ran up to the fifth floor, as fast as my stumpy little

legs allowed. I burst into the room to find—
nothing. I opened the bathroom door, no wife; I
looked in the closet, a bag but no wife; I looked
under the bed, dust but still no wife; I stare at the
ceiling, it stared back. Then, suddenly the
telephone rang. "Come down to operating theatre
3, Now."

Oh my god, something terrible has occurred, I
thought, as I flew down the same steps I had just
flown up. My beloved. As raced around the hall
and there in front of the door to operating theatre
stood a tiny Filipino nurse with her arms akimbo.
I did what any Emile Post would do: I put my
hands under her elbows, lifted her up, pivoted and
put her down so I could run into the room and lend
any assistance that any Walter Mitty with
pretensions could. But when I repivoted, I saw
before me a scene that will haunt me for the rest of
my life. There before me, my spouse lay back in
giant barcolounger with her legs spread,

chitchatting with a perfect stranger who had his head in a place where strangers normally should not put their heads.

Just as I was about to shout:" What the hell is going on here?" another nurse tried to show me something wrapped in swaddling cloth. Now I could try to sugar coat this next painful moment. Lord knows, I had and have all the excuses necessary: early morning, crash, fear and shock. But I will not. The fact is that when I looked into the beautiful face of my new born daughter, besmeared with blood and other red uggies, I said: "Can't you wash her first?"

I UNDERSTAND YOU,
JUST ROAR LOUDER

When my son was just a callowed youth, we both decided that he was at least as intelligent and a great deal more mature than his father. This revelation was the start of the best parent-child relationship since Ham went to tuck Noah in. I left him alone; he left me alone. Since he was an exceptional student and a well-behaved citizen, I accepted the accolades of my peers with a modesty that was totally undeserved and completely insincere.

Of course, there are always snakes in the best of gardens: his mother believed that my brilliant plan for child-rearing was simply the result of my usual sloth so occasionally she insisted I do something she considered actually paternal. When he was about 10, our first, and last, discussion about sex was the result of such gross interference.

We sat across from each other in the den in our respective easy (ha) chairs. I poked the logs in the fire place for an hour or so (I would have poked them longer but it was summer and it became apparent that I was avoiding whatever subject we were forced to discuss). Finally, after extensive throat clearing, I ventured: "Your Mom wants us to talk." I could tell he was as uncomfortable as I with this quaint notion since he crawled under his chair and began whimpering. I could not take anymore: I blurted out," I think the important thing is to follow the advice of the real estate agent who said 'Get a lot while you are young!'" After a pregnant pause, his little head emerged from under the chair to ask," A lot of what?" I responded we would continue this discussion when he was a little older. We left our cave and entered the kitchen like triumphful gladiators to tell all who would listen that we had a father-son talk so profound that it would last us the rest of our lives (if we had anything to say about it)!

You would think that with this background of

monosyllabic masculinity, we could avoid any
further embarrassment, but if so, you do not know
our ability for lower floor self-abasement. A quiet
decade later, a wiser man would have simply
ignored the repeated requests for payment from
Rutgers since the fruit of my loins was attending
Princeton, but oh no, I had to point out the
coincidence of two students with the exact same
name at neighboring universities.

Now in addition to his other virtues my progeny
is an extremely honest person (unlike one of his
parents who regales any one who will listen with
fabrications and falsehoods about his family). He
was clearly embarrassed: he muttered "I have
never misled you and I don't want to start," and
motioned me to join him on the porch. Now we
do not think straight but we sure think fast: in a
nanosecond I had decided that any news that could
only be delivered out of earshot of his beloved
mother was so...so....so shocking, that it had to

concern SEX. Given the closeness that had arisen from our first heart-to-heart (now mercifully edited by time and a failing memory to be an actual discussion), I knew, just knew, that the news could only be revealed to his dear old dad. What news could that be I thought, as I slowly, and I mean slowly, strode to the back door. It could not be academic failure: too early in the semester. It could not be an impending marriage: that was definitely news for his dear old mom. Oh my god, I thought as my palsied hand tried to turn the knob: he is going to reveal he is GAY. And to think I just cut a check to the alumni fund!

This was it I thought: an actual opportunity to do some good. To act like a man (instead of my usual impersonation of a timid mouse). In a trice (actually a twice but who wants to brag), I had composed a speech of such sensitivity that the Gay Pride parade would want to name a float in my honor. I stood on the porch ready to give him a manly hug and assure him of our uninterrupted love, affection and support when the words "Air Force" forced their way through the thick skin of my self-congratulations. "Say again," I muttered.

"I said I joined the Air Force ROTC and the bill is for a ROTC course.

"THE MILITARY! THE MILITARY! We have been pacifists for seven generations!! The military? I thought you were going to tell me you were gay!

"GAY! GAY! Why the hell did you think that?

"THE MILITARY!?! THE MILITARY!?!

"GAY?!? GAY?!?

Well, I do not want to bore you with the rest of that call and response, but to this day the only "conversations" we have had (except perhaps "Pass the peas, please"), is when my darling boy glares at me across the room and mutters "Gay? Gay?"

And to think; it was such a nice speech that I never gave.

POP POP, THE SITTER

Now if there was one job I thought I could do blindfolded with one arm tied behind my back (a position in which I have found myself on more than one embarrassing occasion), it was to be a grandfather.

How hard could it be I asked my beloved daughter-in-law? Heck, I raised two kids and they are perfect (well, not exactly perfect but they did survive to adulthood or at least quasi-adulthood). And if the tough got going, the tough could ship the little brat back to its parents (if that is not the common expression, it sure as heck should be).

I was ready. Indeed, I was eager (although not as eager as somebody who bought ever baby thing ever manufactured in both pink and blue for, as she said, with a goofy smile, "Who knows?").

My first hint that this was to be no stroll in the park was when I was invited into the "birthing room." Now, I don't want to sound like the Neanderthal that I am (particularly first thing in the morning), but in my day women were taken away to some mystic place where, in the glow of angel light, the miracle of birth happened while men read old magazines in disgustingly dirty lobbies and killed each other with second and third hand smoke. When the doctor entered and pulled up the sheet, I fled like a timid doe to the nastiest laughs you could imagine. Their muttered descriptions of my character could not be repeated in a family publication.

OK, so I don't like the "uggie" things. It wasn't that I was needed (or even wanted) at that moment. Indeed, for the next several months my only role seemed to be to hold the little darling for thankfully brief periods of time and accept the accolades of his adoring public ("How cute!!" gushed by elderly ladies is a phrase that should be prohibited under the pain of death (or worse)). But

I knew my day would come. It did.

When my pride and joy (the kid, not the polish or detergent) turned six months, I was given the awesome responsibility of attending his majesty during his afternoon nap. Considering that he usually slept at least two hours and my darling wife and daughter-in-law promised to return in an hour, I was my most confident self (my most confident self unfortunately verges on manic assertiveness that frequently results in harm to my aging body).

Several minutes passed in blessed tranquility. The child snuggled so warmly in his bed, while his beloved grandfather did what he did best- reading the newspaper on the sofa as his eyelids slowly sink beneath the horizon of his bloodshot pupils. Suddenly, I reminded myself that there was no sleeping on this job. Girded by the weight of my responsibility, I trod heavily (actually, I always trod heavily) into the little prince's room so I could report that their faith was not misplaced.

As I stared down at that little cherubic face, I was filled with love. Then two tiny eyes slowly opened and he smirked at me as if I was the tiny mouse and he was the giant cat. My heart stopped, my blood ran cold: I had seen the face of Lucifer himself. The piercing scream that emitted from that tiny mouth would have put a Wagnerian soprano to shame.

When I recovered from my swoon, I leapt into action. I mentally listed the emergency measures that my darling had iterated and reiterated as if I was a not too bright child. I would show her. First, change the diaper. It was the work of a moment to grab the little devil and remove his sleepers. It was the work of a moment to remove his diaper. Oh my God, he pooped!! And, my Lord, it smelled!! I thought that babies emitted clover, or something. How in hell did the brat turn milk into this mess? My kids never made this much of a stench. Then I remembered that I had actually avoided ever changing a diaper for my kinders (got to run to the office was my favorite, even at 2:00AM on Sunday night- I was shameless). By an incredible act of bravery, and by holding my breath until I turned purple, I was able to remove the old diaper, throw the old diaper out of the window and put on a new diaper. I did not wash his smelly butt, having decided that he was too young to deny that he had a second poop after the change.

I returned to the divan mentally and physically exhausted but proud; I had met the enemy and triumphed. Just as I was mentally accepting the accolades of an adoring wife and daughter-in-law, I heard yet another shriek. But I was ready. Second, make him a bottle. Aha. I did so and the wee bugger was ever so grateful. He looked so cute; how could I have misunderstood the petit prince? He sucked down the bottle as if he was a grizzled veteran of Alcoholics Anonymous. Oh well, I could handle another bottle. His lids slowly descended like the wings of a butterfly as I returned to the couch.

The next shriek made the first two shrieks sound like the murmurs of doves: fortunately the sofa was soft and broke my fall. I dashed into his room with the mantra on my lips: Third, burp him gently. You may be surprised to learn that it is impossible to burp an infant without putting his milk smeared mouth on the shoulder of your favorite sweater and his odoriferous behind near your sensitive nose, but it is unfortunately true. I am not, however, a man who shrinks from his responsibilities (although my spouse would disagree, loudly). I gently patted his tiny back until he gave a burp that would have made a college freshman at his first keg party proud.

I returned to my day bed of rest ready for a well-deserved nap. I glanced at my watch and, to my amazement, less than an hour had passed since I was thrown into the jaws of death. Oh well, I had run the gauntlet and I had survived. I could not believe my ears when a few moments later yet another scream rent the house (at that point, I would have rented the house to anyone who would take this spawn of Satan away). I looked at that red-faced little twerp and frantically repeated "Diaper, milk, burp" like it was a magic incantation to summon Mary Poppins.

I was so frantic I even opened his diaper again and changed him when I found water, lots of water. This did not satisfy him for more than a nanosecond. As soon as he opened his yap, I flung him over my shoulder and pounded him until he "ooffed." It worked for me. No, that was not it. I ran into the kitchen and made yet another bottle and tossed him into his crib.

I cannot remember much after that third bottle. Just an endless saga of diaper, bottle and burp, again and again. I felt like the myth of the Sisyphus, endlessly pushing the boulder up the mountain every day and having it roll back every night. Several centuries later I finally heard the sounds of a car pulling into the driveway. I crawled over its sharp pebbles, flung myself at my saviors' knees and whimpered pitifully "Thank God you are home. That monster has been up since you left, I changed him a hundred times and fed him ten gallons of milk and he still will not sleep!! I don't know what to do to shut him up."

They both ran up to his room while I lay down on the sofa with a cold compress over my fevered brow. My dear wife returned and said "I don't know what in the heck you are complaining about. The little precious is sleeping like an angel." And he was. But I know. And he knows I know. Little Precious, indeed.

POP POP'S FIRST SLEEPOVER

Day One

For some reason (which I attribute to divine
justice acknowledging my exemplary goodness),
we have not had the privilege (my son's phrase, I
assure you) of having our darling grandchildren
sleep over in our house until last week.

Our adventure began bright and early one crisp
Fall morning when our beloved daughter-in-law
drove up in a large van to deposit all of the articles
she was sure we would need over the next two
days for her beloved son, aged five going on
thirty, and daughter, one and half going on one
and one half.   As she opened the rear gate, a
cornucopia of toys, the likes of which have never
before been seen south of Santa's workshop,
spilled down around her pleasure-dazed brood.
At my most sympathetic (not very and utterly
insincere), I tried to assure her that her "honey

lambs" would probably survive the trauma of a separation from her for two whole days; with tears cascading down her cheeks like the mighty Niagara: she was certain that in the near future a bevy of behaviorists would be accusing her of egregious child abuse.

Did you ever notice that the fruit of your own loins will toss their fruit at you while driving away but an in-law seems- how can one say it? - less than enthusiastic about your parenting skills? A recent rigorous scientific study (several calls to other grandparents) concluded that the reason for such disparity was simple: every child thinks that he or she is pretty close to perfect so, no matter how stupid their parents were when they were young, the parents must have learned a great deal since then and, therefore, they can be trusted; your in-law has had to live with the result of your parenting skills and has concluded, therefore, that you were obviously lousy parents and cannot be trusted. To prove my point, my daughter-in-law proceeded to filled my arms with reams and reams of detailed instructions so basic (do <u>NOT</u> allow them to use a motorcycle without supervision, NO parachuting) that an unbiased observer would conclude that she was leaving her children in the care of the Three Stooges. I assured her that I understood the importance of early bedtimes, no more than one half hour of non-violent, non-cartoon, family TV and no candy. After I crossed my heart and hoped to die, she finally fled in tears as if she had delivered them to slavery.

 My helpmate, who had been cleverly hiding under our bed, appeared and made me a liar by the simple expedient of stuffing their little mouths with chocolate, filling their little grasping arms with even more presents, and herding them in front of the TV so that they could watch every program expressly forbidden to them in their own home.

Early in our own child rearing days, my wife and I took the most solemn oath to all of the gods and goddesses of marital bliss that we would never, ever, ever, under any circumstances, contradict the other in front of our own little monsters. I cannot say with a straight face that this was a complete success: our children soon learned that when one parent gasped and slapped his or her hand over his or her mouth when the other was handing down yet another edict, it probably meant that the parent of the second part thought the parent of the first part was an idiot and there was room for further negotiations.

So I waited until my bride left the den before pointing out in a voice as gentle as a dulcimer and as conciliatory as a cool breeze in August, that perhaps we should apportion our largesse with a more restrained hand for the sake of discipline and good order (and not scrambling all of our nest eggs as divertimento for the <u>kinder</u>).

I now knew fear: as the last sweet word exited my trembling lips, the temperature plunged thirty degrees, the sky darkened, the sound of distant thunder arose in the East; my treasure stretched to her full five foot two inches and roared through clenched jaws:" Sir, when I was a parent I made Marine Corp sergeants look like slackers but now, now I am a GRANDPARENT and my job, my mission, my calling is to spoil them as they have never been spoiled before!!! And you know why???"

My knees quaked like aspens in a windstorm and I could only shake my lowered head.

"Because, you idiot, I am not responsible. Any tiny flaw is clearly the fault of our in-laws. SO HA!" And with that she turned, dashed back into the den and continued to throw goodies at them as if she was a demented flower girl at a psychedelic wedding.

Strangely enough, her technique seemed to work: peace and harmony prevailed as the little darlings lay on the den floor, besmeared with candy, eyes glazed from a Sponge Bob marathon, and stuffed to satiation with take-out pizza. By 8:00 PM, the wee nippers were so deeply asleep that we could carry them to their beds, change their undergarments and unceremoniously dump them in their beds without hearing a murmur of protest.

As we gazed over the ruins of our family room like the survivors of trench warfare peeking at no-man's land, I turned to my spouse and said the words that really make woman weak at the knees and swoon with desire:" You were right and I was wrong. Your grand parenting skills even exceed your remarkable parenting skills."

Day Two

My smugness only increased about 3:00 AM when the little angel need her diaper changed. Following strict instructions, I changed her quickly, without comment or eye contact, and she went back to sleep as predicted. Maybe my son and daughter-in-law did know something. When she began crying at 4:37AM, I found her diaper dry, and made the fatal error of asking "What is wrong, darling?" Perhaps you have the intestinal fortitude to deny a blond haired, blue eyed cherub when she lifts her arms and coos "Up, PopPop" but I did not.

As a result of this act of mercy, I spent the next three hours trying to amuse a one year old without waking the rest of the family. If you do not mind carpets covered with "amber waves of grain", a large, very large bowl of rice crispies will keep a one and a half year old fed and amused for at least

20 seconds. Only a mere two hours, fifty nine minutes and forty seconds until I can wake my bride without fear of divorce, I thought.

They say that the difference between a test pilot and us ordinary folks is that when an experimental plane is hurdling to earth, the test pilot remains calms and cool. Ha, let those leather-clad, walrus mustached macho men try to amuse a baby at four in the morning: their blood pressure will shoot up like geysers in Yellowstone Park.

Time, Einstein said, is dependent upon the observer: I can attest to that as the next few hours passed with the speed of an arthritic tortoise. I have vague memories of a dairy of milk cups, a mountain of diapers, endless reels of Japanese cartoons, a city of building blocks and more games of Ring Around the Rosie than were played during the Black Death, all interspersed with "SSSSSSShhhhhh", Grandma and your brother are sleeping."

When they found me at sunrise, it was not a pretty site or sight: they say that Hercules would have taken a lifetime to clean our den so it took my Duchess a mere hour to find me under a pile of diapers, blocks, and empty milk cups and lead me to well earned nap.

When I awoke it was time to pick up my grandson from school. Being not a complete idiot, I gave him the latest edition of Zagat's and the choice of any fine dining establishment for lunch: after deliberate reflection, he chose a restaurant whose name will not be mentioned, ever again. When the plastic toy is the only edible morsel in the gaily colored box, you should probably refer to yourself as a toy store and not as a restaurant, but he was happy so my cramps were a mere peccadillo as we all drove home.

Now, as we all know, there are slight exaggerations, fibs, white lies and outright frauds. The statement," Don't worry, she takes a three hour nap every day after lunch like clockwork" seems, in retrospect, to be closer to the latter than the former. Dimples, as my granddaughter is occasionally called, held up a book, "One Fish, Two Fish", gave me the full winsome treatment and a pathetic cry of "PopPop" so I began to read her to sleep.

When I awoke, I discovered that a grown man can fit in a crib although I cannot say how: all I know is that my wife did not find this at all amusing. "What the hell are you doing?" was in fact what she said. I had no answer. I was tired. I consulted my watch: only one hour until the PARENTS, as we now referred to our formerly beloved son and that person he married through clenched teeth.

If I had thought that time passed slowly at 4 in the morning, I can now assure you that it does not pass at all when you are waiting for the PARENTS to arrive when they damn well promised to arrive: BEFORE, not after dinner.

While I am known principally for my sweet disposition, I am also known as a man who rarely digresses: straight talk and a straight story I always say. But I must stop to observe the fact that the worse you are as a parent, the less you have to do as a grandparent. So I guess it is a compliment when your child calls to chuckle at your distress that he is stopping for dinner (and will be hours later than promised): "Ha, ha. I know you and the kids will be fine." Oh yeah, if I had beaten you, you would not be so damned sure, I thought.

In addition to my straight as an arrow nature, I am a man who is sensitive, emphatically empathetic, some have said. In a nanosecond (or less) I noticed that my object of my affection, who normally makes Martha Stewart look like trailer trash after a particularly bad night, had begun to show alarming cracks in her own façade. She was actually brushing her golden hair from her eyes with a used diaper to enable her to affix me with a stare that Medusa would envy. "My plum, is something wrong?" I inquired in tones calculated to melt the hardest heart.

"Wrong, wrong? You big ape. All you have done all day is take naps while I have cooked, cleaned and changed filthy diapers for YOUR grandchildren." Now my memory, like various other parts of my anatomy, is definitely slipping, but I distinctly remember early in our married life a similar phrase ("MY" children, as I recall), usually immediately before the mask of civilization slipped from her beautiful, albeit stressed face, and she attacked me like a crazed banshee unless I immediately removed myself and "my" children from her sight.

You know that sitting on the front porch so your grandchildren can catch fireflies has many, many joys: that of recollecting your own childhood; that of remembering your children when they were adorable; and that of getting the hell out of the house. In addition, when your child finally pulls his car in your driveway and finds you and his children on the front porch with a giant glass jar filled with fireflies, he will be under the mistaken impression that you are a loving and attentive grandfather who can be trusted to take care of his children at any time and for any length of time: Who says that no good deed ever goes….oh, you know.

POP POP BUILDS A DREAM
HOUSE

I heard her gasp; then her heart beat faster (and louder). Once I thought I was the cause (in my youth, I even thought I was the cure, but that is another, sadder story); now I knew that it had always been the Joy of Shopping.

I whirled around in the vast toy emporium (and around), and reminded her of her recent pledges, beginning with "Let's not go crazy this birthday. I don't want to spoil him." Then I saw what she was looking at: a jungle gym, no, a jungle city, that soared to the ceiling and sprawled across the floor in a calliope of swings and slides and ladders and bars. Somewhere in the jungles of New Guinea I sensed that a family of twenty-four was building a similar structure for all of them to live in together, but smaller, much smaller.

"Are you nuts?" I asked rhetorically (has anyone ever answered "Yes"? And if they do, does that prove that they're aint?). "He'll be three, a little kid. You would have to be the entire Von Trapp family to justify that metropolis." She looked through me as if I did not exist. Her eyes glistened as she imagined her grandchild in the red, white and blue of the US Olympic Acrobatic Team leaping like an inspired gazelle, to the envy of the other neighborhood urchins and her less fortunate friends.

"No, no, no," I thundered. Never, never, never," I roared. "Please, please don't," I whimpered. Her lips said, "Of course not, it is too big and too expensive." But I heard her heart crooning, "Yes, yes, yes. Just wait my little darling!" Sure enough, four days later, my son, the soul of restraint and reticence when it comes to his own money (which rarely goes), invited us to Saturday dinner, beginning at 8:00 AM (and bring your drill).

Now a normal man, an oxymoron in itself (which

term, parenthetically, originated when my wife's Scandinavian ancestor, Ollie Moronson, nicknamed the "Ox", told his wife that men could be "considerate lovers" if only their wives would stop giving directions), would be highly suspicious at such an invitation (did you remember where we were?), but, I thought, "If you can't trust your kids, who could you trust (none, it turned out)."

Bright and early (more early than bright, actually), I arrived at my progeny's manse just as an 18-wheeler slightly larger than the Queen Mary was backing up into his driveway. As I watched in awe, a crack team of native bearers began to carry boxes on their heads into the back yard while merrily chanting "Go asao uaha yi, yi, yi " (which means "At least we don't have to put the damn thing together, ha, ha, ha!").

My formerly beloved child grinned at me and said,

with an almost straight face, "I knew that you would want to help build your own present." A lesser man would have flung himself on the palisade of boxes and described, in vivid detail, the poor house for which he was destined; I comforted myself with the thought of the reading of my last Will. "Your Father, a man of incredible generosity and unparalleled love, after a life time of indulging a spendthrift wife and profligate children, died without a sou. Sou sorry."

We began by opening all of the boxes and throwing all of the directions in the trash. Like all real men, we consider reading instructions to be a sure sign of a misspent youth or an effete maturity. We then, of course, began to weld, solder, screw, bolt or nail anything that remotely seemed to go together while reassuring each other with the mantra of the terminally unhandy:"Looks right to me!"

As the day wore on, and on, and on, and the sun rose while our spirits set, cheerful reassurances were replaced with muttered imprecations through clenched teeth: "Didn't you measure that? I thought you measured it!!"

Just as the sun and the temperatures reached their zeniths, Der Alte began to swoon from his Herculean labors (and no lunch). In my delirium, I swore I saw the other slaves trying to lift the gigantic stones up the pyramids as the cruel taskmaster (who had an uncanny resemblance to my flesh and blood) whipped them without mercy.

"What are you and PopPop doing?" the birthday boy piped up. "Just getting your inheritance early," my son cackled in maniacal glee. But such slurs against my manhood and the working conditions of an Alabama chain gang simply spurred this construction stud to new heights of exertion. Finally, several millennia later, I held the last nut (no comments if you please) while my progeny tightened the last bolt.

And the little darling almost made it all worth while (almost) by saying, "You can have the slide first, PopPop."

THE TWITS

Every family has them: the snotty ones. You know what I mean. The ones who read the New York Times book reviews to impress you but never the books themselves. The ones who subscribe to many magazines but rarely read any of them. The ones who didn't quite succeed but are making damn sure that their children will whether they want to or not. We have one set of twits in my family whose names will be cleverly changed to avoid harm to the author. As proof of their twitiness, the following is a copy of one of their letters without editorial comment (except perhaps a snicker or two).

"Dear Abby:

My wife and I have a problem that we simply cannot talk about with our family or friends so we are turning to you for advice.

I should begin by telling you that my wife and I live in a medium-sized city in the Northeast. We are both teachers in our local high school: I teach English and I am the head of our drama department; she teaches art and runs the dance program. The subject of our concern is Dylan, our only child, who is a senior in our school.

Let me emphasize that no parents have ever done as much for a child as we have done for Dylan. As soon as my wife knew she was pregnant, she never went to bed without placing a speaker on her belly so Dylan could hear classical music at the earliest possible time. As soon as he was born, his crib had a mobile of great works of art. As soon as he began to show his remarkable talent for art in kindergarten, we gave up vacations so he could have private lessons. While other children received toys and video games, we were careful to choose only those things that would advance his aesthetic education.

Perhaps we could be criticized by others less interested in their children's development but, based upon our attempt to "make it" in New York when we graduated from our local colleges, we knew that there was little chance for Dylan unless he had an orientation consistent with his talent. Therefore, unlike other parents, we were willing to ignore our normal predilections for his ultimate benefit. Despite my deepest desire to bond with my first born, I refused to play baseball or football or any sport with him, pretending that a bad back would not allow such activities. Instead of such manly activities, Dylan was sent to ballet class. At home, he was asked to help with the cooking and taught to sew.

As Dylan approached his adolescent years we made what I thought was the ultimate sacrifice: despite a lifetime of the philosophic smugness that comes with advanced agnosticism, we joined a local born-again church which believed that the ultimate sin was homosexuality. We knew that children eventually rebelled against their parents' beliefs and we wanted to give Dylan a specific target.

Notwithstanding our sacrifices, we noticed certain alarming trends as he grew older. Last month we caught him with binoculars peeking in the bedroom of the girl next door. Yesterday, he announced that he was asking that slut to his Senior Prom. I guess by now you have realized our dark and terrible secret: our son, our beloved son, has chosen a life style antithetical to our hopes for his future as a great artist- Dylan is straight. Despite the art lessons, the ballet lessons, the cooking classes and the other hundred things we did and refrained from doing, he seems to be decidedly heterosexual.

We are at our wit's end. Do we confront him? Do we try to persuade him that our hopes and dreams will come to naught if he persists in his normality? Please write as soon as possible. The prom is in one week."

MY COUSIN TIMMY

Great achievements, like beauty, are definitely in the eye of the beholder.

My cousin Timmy is a nice enough guy but he is one of the dullest people in my entire family, if not in the world. When we were growing up, he was so quiet we all thought he was one of the kids we now referred to as special. Imagine my surprise when my Aunt Britt proudly told me at some family function that Timmy had been admitted to a reasonably decent law school. Several years late, I was shocked to hear from my Uncle Allen that Timmy was working at a pretty good, local law firm.

Several years ago, I was walking on Main Street in our little town when I bumped into Timmy. We had to chit chat to be polite, of course, and he told me that he was working in the estates department of his law firm, writing wills and the like. No great surprise there: a natural simpatico between Timmy and the dead, the only group less exciting than my dear cousin.

Last Christmas, I was at my Uncle Allen's house for a family party and who attaches himself to me like a drowning barnacle but my cousin Timmy. He wants to tell me a story.

Now I did not know it- and apparently neither did Timmy although he had been in practice for more than ten years- that in our State lawyers are assigned to represent indigent criminals pro bono, that is for free. Timmy just found this out from a very, very irritated bureaucrat who yelled at him that ALL attorneys meant ALL attorneys, even estate lawyers who know as much about criminal law as Dick Chaney knows about peaceful coexistence. The bureaucrat was irritated because the lack of demand for Timmy's talents was not the result of his complete and total ignorance of criminal law but the result of this bureaucrat entering the wrong address for Timmy in their records when he graduated law school.

Timmy told me that he begged and pleaded to be excused. According to him, his eloquence rivaled Brutus at

Caesar's funeral, Lincoln at Gettysburg and Jesus on the Mount but to no avail. The bureaucrat did say, "don't worry, I'll take care of you," so Timmy was hoping for a traffic ticket dispute or something along those lines. A week later Timmy swooned when he opened a large package from the bureau and found that he was assigned to defend a triple murderer.

The day before Tim was scheduled to visit his "client" in the county jail, he checked that his Will was up to date, called his mother and hugged and kissed his wife with more passion than French aristocrats showed when boarding a tumbrel for a ride to the guillotine. The day of the interview, he drove slowly, very slowly, to the county jail but was quickly ushered into what the guard referred to as an "interview room." The interview room was a dimly-lit, 8x10 closet, attractively finished with poop brown tile, and furnished only with an aluminum table and two aluminum chairs. The only connection to the outside world was a teeny, tiny window inset in a thick steel door.

When the guard finally brought the prisoner in, Timmy admitted he audibly gasped. His "client" was no more than 5' 6" in height but he was at least 6' in width with muscles so gigantic that the buttons on his shirt hung on for dear life. He had a small, shaven bullet shaped head, and a neck that sloped down to shoulders so massive that deltoid implants seemed possible. Timmy was not ashamed to admit that he gave besieging looks to the guard in the hope that he would remain, even though the guard looked about twelve years old and would run like a startled deer in the event of trouble, but the guard left as soon as the monster was seated.

Timmy said that there was only two things he could recall about the interview The first was that King Kong told him that he had killed two guys in Florida so "I don't need no fucken lawyer. If I beat the rap here, they'll just send me back for a lethal." The second was that ogre proudly admitted that he had killed the "Jersey guy" because the "little fucker" had the nerve to question whether he had the balls to shoot two guys in Florida. "I guess the mother fucker knows now," the troll chuckled. Just as Timmy was going to pound on the door, the monster provided absolute proof of a benign and loving god: he demanded that Timmy plead him guilty so he would be sentenced in a state unfortunately without capital punishment and, as he eloquently stated, "Florida could then kiss my lily white ass." Timmy nodded his agreement and left without a backward glance.

So I said to Timmy it seemed to me that there was a happy ending to this too, too long saga. Timmy thought for a moment and said yes, but only because he had the opportunity to dazzle the court with the brilliance he never knew he had. I asked how he could have dazzled the court if there has been no trial since mighty joe young was pleading guilty. My cousin said there had been no trial, but there had been a hearing for sentencing for which he was required to appear. So how did he dazzle, I asked. He said that the hearing was perfunctory until a large bleached blond in a small skirt, with makeup that had been troweled on her tough face, stood up in the middle of the hearing and announced, in a thick North Jersey accent, that she wanted to say something. Timmy said he could not help himself: due entirely to his watching hundreds of episodes of Law and Order, he actually stood up and objected (your honor, the lady is not a participant to these proceedings) but the judge allowed her to make a statement. It seemed that the Ann Nicole look-alike wanted the judge to sentence her former boyfriend to death in the most painful method possible. When the judge explained that New Jersey did not execute criminals she argued, rather eloquently according to Timmy, that that if any one ever deserved to die it was that "son of a bitch." Timmy said that it was his one moment of glory: he immediately stood, repeated his objection and asked that the remarks be stricken form the record and the judge said "I agree with Counsel for the Defendant and order the remarks stricken." At that moment, Timmy decided that the criminal bar had probably lost the next Clarence Darrow when he chose to represent the dead and the soon to be deceased.

I congratulated Timmy but as he was leaving I realized that if I could not share his joy in his "achievement", at least there was a moral to this tale. The moral is that there would be a hell of a lot less crime if all potential wrongdoers knew that they would be defended <u>pro bono</u> by such as my cousin Timmy.

MY COUSIN GARY

It is difficult for even the most intelligent person to decide whether a particular characteristic is the result of genetics or the environment. My paternal family was well known both for their intelligence and for their inability to do anything useful with such a gift. Their natural state was one of confusion as they used their blessing to see every alternative until the chance to do anything about it had long passed. If a family member of mine had stood on the peaks of Darien and gazed at the Pacific instead of Cortez, he would have taken one absent-minded step forward and plunged to his death.

Yet, I believe that my cousin Gary's natural state of addlepateness was the result of his upbringing rather than the upbringers. He was not raised in the state of denial, as so many have thought, but in a home of hugger-muggers. I can give you many examples, but perhaps one will do.

When Gary was very young, five or six perhaps, he heard, in the background of noise that children are surrounded with, his grandparents talking about a neighbor who had suddenly grown so rich that they could afford a "svatza." Now, we were raised in an era that did not look back on the Old Country with nostalgia; to the contrary, all of our grandparents wanted their children and grandchildren to be Americans first, last and always; to shed all of the old customs as soon as possible, including a language other than English. It was more than a little ironic that they thought that a child who said "mudder", "fadder" and "toity toid street" was actually speaking impeccable English.

But Gary had picked up enough of their lingo to know that "svartz" meant black and a "svartza" probably meant a black person. According to my cousin he was instantly transfixed: at last, something exotic was coming to his dull, lower middle class neighborhood heretofore populated by persons who were only colorful when red from drink or rage. Being a prodigious reader, Gary had come across black people in books, and, to a man, or women, they were like peacocks compared to my friends and family: dressed in rich, colorfully clothing and surrounded by lions and the like. Now he was about to meet a person who was black, a "svatza": he could hardly wait. Who knew, today a svartza, tomorrow a tiger or an elephant?

For the next few days, Gary changed his after-school stoop ball locale from his home at 154 McKenzie Street to 141 McKenzie Street, in front of the now palatial home of the newly wealthy. He patiently threw his old spaldeen against the stoop again and again until some adult suggested, in the dulcet tones that one Brooklynite uses to address another: "Get the f___ out of here you little s___ or I'll stick that ball up your a__." He reluctantly departed.

But game guy that he was, he returned again and again. No walk was complete without a detour in front of 141. No errand could be taken without him passing this now fantastic fortress of mystery. And then one day his fortitude was rewarded: the door opened, and a middle-aged woman stepped out carrying a broom with which she proceeded to sweep the steps.

Gary said he was crushed. She was not black at all. At best, she was a light beige, a coffee with three creams. What a gyp. Heck, he pointed out that we had an uncle who, at least in the summer, was a hell of a lot darker than the so-called "svartza." Slowly Gary walked back to his house, head down, dragging his feet and scuffing his new Keds. Of course, he was confused. Heck he had been misled, misinformed and lead astray so it was no wonder that during his early youth he was puzzled, perplexed and disconcerted. He had been promised Ringling Brothers and Barnum Bailey Circus and all he got was our Aunt Molly singing "Wanted." Socks instead of the big Tinker Toy kit, the one that you could build the parachute ride in Coney Island. In his humble opinion, he believed that a permanent twist had been inflicted on his DNA that day.

Of course you will point out, in tones of sweet reasonableness, that everyone has had similar experiences and many of them grew up in the best of mental health. But that was just one of a series that lead to my cousin' present, unsettled state of mind.

Gary's best friend at the time was Catholic kid named Patrick. They were inseparable except during school hours as he was bused to a nearby parochial school and Gary walked to the public school around the corner from his house.

When they met after school, they never discussed school. They both hated school. They talked about baseball teams, pro wrestlers, comic books and touch football or sand lot soft ball, depending upon the season. The big kids bullied the small kids and the small kids bullied the smaller kids and all was right in his world. No adults and no adult concerns.

Gary told me that a few years after the svatza incident, as he dubbed it, Gary's buddy began to tell his some disturbing things he learned in his parochial school. The first bombshell he dropped on Gary was that after Gary died, he would go to hell and burn there forever. It seems that a member of Gary's family killed a member of Patrick's family a long time ago. Then he told Gary that that member of his family was actually a member of his family but something happened so they were pissed off at each other. For quite a time, poor Gary could not walk without periodically spinning around to make sure that no one was out to get him because of our homicidal ancestors. Gary, already "puzzled, perplexed and disconcerted", was forced to conclude that here was another mystery that he was unable to solve and further proof that whatever he was, it was not "captain of his ship or master of his soul."

Then Patrick's older brothers started sex-ed classes and now he had tales that really scared the hell out of Gary or disgusted the hell out of him or both. First, it was do you know where babies come from? Of course Gary didn't! In our family, sex was a subject that never, ever was discussed in front of the"children." Patrick swore that the deal was that your mother eats more and more until she has a stomach like your Uncle Morty, then she goes to the bathroom and comes out with a baby. Patrick was quite vague as to the details but that was quite enough for Gary who began to watch his mother eat and grew horrified whenever she decided to have seconds. The poor kid was convinced that every bite was the beginning of another, and very unwanted, sibling? It was not, of course, but it was the confirmation of a world that conspired to induce neuroses in the weakened minded.

The final nails in the cross of consternation upon which my cousin was hung were Patrick's tales of sins and confession. His brothers must have loved telling their little brothers of matters that they themselves do not understand and never experienced. The head of a Jewish household is supposed to relate the story of his people leaving Egypt to each of his children in a form that is suited to their age and capacity. Patrick relating the stories of sin and redemption was like the evil child (his older brother) relating the Exodus story to the simple child (Patrick)who then relates it to the child "who hath no capacity to inquire" (Gary, of course).

His first story was of "jerking off"; a sin
guaranteed to send you to hell forever, although
Patrick was not entirely sure what it was except it
had something to do with your pee pee. It
probably had a different effect on Patrick and his
older brothers but, in Gary's case, in an abundance
of caution, he ceased looking at his pee pee when
he whizzed and, as a result, his bathroom began to
resemble a pissoire in a bikers' bar.

Between Gary's new habits of periodically
spinning around when out of the house and not
looking below the waist while in the house, he was
clearly destined to join the ranks of the terminally
affected if not afflicted. But that was not even the
beginning of his initiation into a neurotic
adulthood. Oh, no, not by a long shot because
then Patrick began to bring home tales of sins of
the flesh with girls, a subject heretofore limited to

booger jokes and sly but puzzled glances at the unusually well-endowed.

Gary said he was always jealous of Catholic kids. Like kids raised on a farm who could always watch a couple of animals couple if they were confused, the nuns gave those parochial school kids a real head start. Who would even think of sticking your tongue down someone's throat without first being told it was a sin and therefore something all of the girls wanted to do as soon as they could find a willing tongue? The same for masturbation, fornication and all of the other stuff the parents and grandparents in our family would never mentioned.

I laughed at these stories and told Gary that he should not make too much of these childhood traumas but my poor cousin insisted that the effects were permanent and profound. He insisted that, to this very day, he cannot enter into a doctor's office, or a sexual relation, without a shudder as the ghost of a gigantic and grotesque sister of the cloth gently chides him for his misdeeds.

RAISING CAIN (AND ABEL)

In any family, there are differing viewpoints and opinions. The only difference in large families, like mine, is that there are so many, many different viewpoints and opinions that any expression by one relative is sure to be treated as a declaration of war by another relative.

One of the topics that divided my family into warring classes more discordant than the so-called red and blue states, was the efficacy of "spank" versus the "discuss" in rearing children.

The "spank" camp, led by my Uncle Dick (a name some thought as particularly descriptive) believed that "sparing the rod spoils the child" and whumps his little ones secure in the knowledge that he is "doing it for their own good." Another uncle, who will not be named, quoted the biblical "foolishness is bound in the heart of a child but the rod of correction shall it far from him" (ignoring, of course, the mercy and turning the other cheek bits in the later testament) and beat the devil out of his children every time he thought he heard God so command. Most of the hitters I am happy to say consisted of occasional smackers on the butt who then felt so guilty that a trip to the local ice cream emporium was required.

The "discuss" side, led by my Aunt Evie, was equally adamant that "it takes a loving village to raise a child" and talked and talked and talked to their wee ones even when their tiny eyes glaze over and they repeated their transgressions again and again. The other talkers ranged from those who lectured others on the evils of physical punishment and would not hit their little darlings if they burned down their houses with their other parent inside to those whose philosophy did not stand in the way of a pinched ear or other means of showing extreme displeasure.

The "spankers" clique sneered at the "discussers" and wonder out loud why they cannot tell the difference between adults and children; the discussers" responded with horror at people who used their children as punching bags to deal with their deep-rooted emotional problems.

Although I have an undeserved reputation of never missing the opportunity to throw gasoline on an open fire, I did not join in the debate for I had observed in my own home that if the house was filthy, your mother-in-law was on her way and you have told your prides and joys to please put away their toys (and no, do not take out another thing) for the umpteenth time: even the bluest of the "blue staters" turns red and smacks him or her on whatever you can reach. On the other hand, it is easier to give a "time out" then to deal with the little one telling his or her Grammy that Mommy or worse Daddy hit me (complete with waterworks and sobs).

Finally, the patriarch of our family, a man better known for a complete lack of patience than for diplomacy, wiped the drool from his quivering lips, and ended the debate by drowning out the others with the following advice.

"What you idiots fail to understand is that your ability to change the behavior of your children is ZIP, NADA,

NOTHING. That's right. Look around you. There are kids who were beaten like drums who turned out to be Noble Prize winners (and who adore their parents, the beaters). There are kids who were raised in the most loving households imaginable whose faces now grace the 10 Most Wanted posters in your local post office. And vice versa."

"So relax. Be happy. Do what you want, when you want secure in the knowledge that it is only your needs and desires that you can, and should fulfill. Feel like hitting, hit. Feel like playing the saint, smile and discuss. Do both; it will keep them confused and on their little toes."

Both factions sat with their mouths agog and their chins resting on their chests. Finally, one of my more pompous cousins, a high school teacher with pretensions, muttered "How could he expect us to live with such hypocrisy. How could we face our friends and collegues?"

"LIE ABOUT IT", my grandfather replied. "If what we

do makes no difference, then you can say anything you want, when you want, and to whom you want. When your boss's wife, who I know looks like Tugboat Annie but not as elegant, brags how she never had to discipline little Faunteroy, you can, and should, smile sweetly and murmur, "I couldn't agree more" (as opposed to pointing out that he is renown as a lying little weasel who tortures small animals). When the bored-again bore down the street boasts that his child is a model for all because of his strict regimen, smile sweetly and murmur, "I couldn't agree more" (as opposed to pointing out that at the age of nine his little boy pees in his pants, undoubtedly also due to the "strict regimen")."

"So congratulations. Not only are you now free from the bounds of social conventions, your stress level will decrease rapidly, and your ability to say what everyone wants to hear will undoubtedly lead to your attaining high political office."

And with that the old man arose, pinched one of his nieces on her butt, and departed to the stunned silence of my family and my deepest admiration.

THIS MORNING

So I'm standing in the john this morning doing what every man does as soon as he wakes up and I notice that my feet are wet. Now I'm at that an age where strange things are becoming rather commonplace. I could have missed and sprayed my feet; it wouldn't surprise me at all. I could be doing it towards the ceiling, convinced that it was raining. Well, not likely now, perhaps, but coming soon (a phrase that, by the way, does no longer means what it once did, just like me).

After eliminating the interesting, to paraphrase Sherlock Holmes, nothing remained but the prosaic. And it was. A leak had developed (if that is the correct term for anything other than a photograph) under my bathroom sink. Quick as an old flash, I threw a good towel on the floor, while having an imaginary conversation with my beloved of five hundred years explaining the emergency and begging forgiveness for so misusing a good towel, and turned the cute little handle under the sink until the water should have stopped. "Aha", I cried in triumph. Then "Oh no, in despair as the leak changed from a gentle drip to an ominous drumbeat. It was if the old family dog had suddenly begun to growl at you. Fear leant grace and agility to my aged frame as I leapt down the cellar steps to grab a large, red bucket. I scampered up the stairs. And scampered down again when I discovered that this large bucket was too large to fit under this tiny sink.

I do not want to break the mood of the moment (or the moment of the mood) but I must interrupt myself (which many have tried and few have succeeded) to explain that my bathroom is a small, ill-lit hovel in an otherwise comfortable abode. When we moved in, there were two bathrooms off of the master bedroom. My bride, a woman of rare beauty as well as the most gracious creature who ever lived, said: "Which bathroom do you want. The ill-lit hovel to the left or the large, luxurious, marble trimmed palace of sybaritic splendor to the right." I said "To the right". My dearest purred" Are you sure you don't want the one to the right. I replied, "I said to the right!" She smiled sweetly and said "Thank you. You are always welcome in my large, luxurious, marble trimmed palace of sybaritic splendor, just take a shower first." I knew that once again rose petal had beaten the tar out of the thorn.

But that was not in my thoughts this morning (although I note that no leak had ever had the nerve to desecrate the large, luxurious, marble trimmed palace of sybaritic splendor of my spouse). My thoughts were of cut-off valves and other manly things. For, in all modesty, I must point out that among my lawyer, doctor, dentist and accountant friends, I am known as the "go-to" guy when it came to home repairs. Indeed, my large and well appointed workshop is the envy of all as well as my favorite retreat (and that is the right word, thank you very much).

"No mere drip will defeat this drip", I vowed. I quickly strapped on my manly tool belt. I unstrapped my manly tool belt even more quickly when I realized that I was clad only in a wet pair of skivvies (with dancing bears of purple and red; "But they were on sale", a statement that brings tears to my eyes and purple bears into my house). It was but the work of a moment to adorn myself with an Allen wrench, monkey wrench, open-end wrench, closed end wrench, partially agape wrench, Stillson wrench, wedge of Stilton cheese and a small screwdriver. I was prepared!

As I marched into my bathroom, I heard the faint strains of the "paso doble" as the courageous matador marched into the bullring to face certain death and knew the kinship of the doomed. My beloved interrupted my revere by quietly pointing out that if Noah had moved as fast as me, Genesis would have been a much shorter book (and that I was an idiot). Anxious to redeem myself in the eyes of my pet, I looked under the sink and saw that water was pouring from the little thingie that goes from the spigot to the pipe in the wall (everyone was quite impress by my facile use of the erudite terms known only to master plumbers). It is difficult to maintain my usual modesty in the face of triumph but I must admit that by turning the doohickey over the leak, I actually reduced the biblical flood to a mere trickle.

The glow of my achievement was dimmed by the voice of my treasure asking, "That's it?" "There's more?" I shot back in astonishment. "It is still leaking!" she tersely pointed out. "But not as much; much, much less!" I murmured. "So what, it is still leaking. What are we going to do? Have a perpetual bucket brigade?" she muttered as she called the plumber.

Several hours later, as Bob the Plumber was putting his tools in his truck, he turned to me and said "Hell of a job you did for an amateur." Aha, I thought. He's a man. He understood. I walked back into the house, my head up, to the faint strains of the "paso doble."

SICKNESS UNTO DEATH

I have noticed that whatever conditions, illnesses, afflictions or diseases members of your family had when you were a child become your standard of normality when you grow up. Unfortunately, every member of my family seems to fall into one of only two categories. The women lived to their late nineties in robust health and died in bed with smirks of smug satisfaction for lives lived long and well. The men died in their fifties, at work, clutching their chests in shocked disbelief at their bodies' betrayal and dismay that there was so much left undone. It is true that one uncle, twice removed, died of tertiary syphilis but that was always considered a moral rather than a physical failing.

As a result of my childhood experiences, I thought that Shakespeare was just being a big sissy when he wrote of the "thousand natural shocks that flesh is heir to." Heck, just avoid doctors, I believed, and you will either die young and make a good looking corpse or you will die old and bore everyone else to death. And this philosophy of avoidance served me well for many, many years. No one prodded or poked me in places that one does not want to be prodded or poked; no waiting in badly decorated rooms filled with old magazines and sick people; no one telling me how to live or diet; no money wasted on expert opinions I'd rather not hear. But, of course, there is always a serpent in every garden of eden; imagine my surprise to find that my snake was none other than my beloved son. I had always assumed that he would be so grateful for my helping him with tuition to medical school that he would simply confirm my idiotic notions. But no. He not only suggested procedures that "a man of your age should have" but the little rat enlisted his mother in his campaign to make me live longer. I can only assume that his motive as a desire to continue to harass me for as long as possible.

After a particular heart-rending series of pleas and inducements, including grisly photographs of men who did not listen to their physicians, I finally agreed to undergo what I referred to as the procedure that "dare not speak its name." According to him, while the fasting the

previous day could be annoying, it could only improve
my rotund body and introduce the concept of sacrifice to
my soul, the procedure itself would be "a price of cake."
In less then it takes to tell this long-winded story, I
entered the hospital and was converted from an upright,
fully clothed adult into a tottering relic whose butt was
exposed to the weather and prying eyes. From a member
of the community whose opinions were occasionally
sought (although rarely accepted) I was reduced to a
codger who had to …be …spoken …to… slowly…in
words of one syllable…but loudly..AS IF I HAD LOST
BOTH INTELLECT AND HEARING. If I protested or
asked for an explanation, the caregiver would simply
repeat what she or he just said but even more
…..slowly….. and …..even…..LOUDER.

The only thing the little twerp was right about was that
modern anesthesia is both swift and sure: I remember
nothing from the time I was injected in the ready room to
the time I opened my beady eyes about an hour or so
later. While I was still on a gurney, I felt fine. Indeed, I

felt great. I had just had the best nap since my grandmother laid me down with a bottle and a teddy bear. With the patience that has made my name famous in Buddhist meditation circles, I removed the tubes from my arms and began to dress. I got as far as my shirt when a nurse as large as Tugboat Annie and as mean as a conservative politician pulled back the curtain and bellowed "Where the hell do you think you are going?" "Home" I responded in a perky voice not heard since Debbie Reynolds retired, cleverly figure

ing that if I sounded well I would be treated as well and allowed to leave. I was not. "You vill wait until your doctor discharges zu." I am ashamed to admit that after carefully looked at her Paul Bunyan like arms, I waited, and waited and waited. Finally, I was told that a polyp or two had been found and removed. Yippee, I thought what could be less scary than a "polyp": sounds like a character in a Disney movie with mermaids. So I went home with a song in my heart and the sure and certain knowledge that I would never see the surgeon or Tugboat Annie again.

My stupidity never ceases to amaze me. Everyone wants to be the best at something. Can I help it if my forte seems to be the utterly fatuous belief that bad things only happen to other people? About a week later my normal obliviousness again collided with reality when my surgeon called to relate the results of the pathology report. Who knew that a report about me was being prepared? Our conversation was brief and not very interesting except for three things. First, I discovered that I had developed an interesting hearing loss: every time he uttered a word beginning with the letter "C", I could not hear the rest of the word. Second, although I had previously rehearsed my reaction to bad news (a studied indifference combined with faint amusement that anyone would make a fuss about such an inevitable part of life), my actual reaction was the lowering of my internal temperature to zero combined with the inability to say anything but "Huh?" Third, I had won another trip to the hospital for a "minor additional procedure."

I remember even less about my hospital stay than the previous "outpatient surgery." When I awoke about 3:00 AM, I did notice that someone had inserted a tube in my most private of private parts. I was determined to repair my self image. I talked the night nurse into removing the tube. Then I leaped (actually tottered) to the bathroom and took a shower, washed my hair and shaved my graying stubble. I changed my backless gown for jeans, a sweatshirt and sneakers. At 6:00AM, a resident finally appeared, looked at me and asked "Where's the patient?" Ha, I thought: "down but not out." And ain't those words to live by and by.

THE END

www.ingramcontent.com/pod-product-compliance
Lightning Source LLC
Chambersburg PA
CBHW061722020426
42331CB00006B/1040